D0319861

MAKING FRIENDS

By Steffi Cavell-Clarke

©2017
Book Life
King's Lynn
Norfolk PE30 4LS

ISBN: 978-1-78637-066-2

Written by:
Steffi Cavell-Clarke

Edited by:
Charlie Ogden

Designed by:
Natalie Carr

A catalogue record for this book
is available from the British Library.

CONTENTS

Words that look like **this** can be found in the glossary on page 24.

WHAT ARE OUR VALUES?

Values are ideas and beliefs that help us to work and live together in a **community**. Values teach us how to behave and how we should **respect** each other and ourselves.

Respecting others

Making your own choices

Understanding different faiths

Being responsible

Our Values

Helping others

Sharing your ideas

Respecting the law

Listening to others

5

OUR FRIENDS

Many people have friends. We can have friends at home, at school and in our community. Our friends are people who we **trust** and enjoy spending time with.

Our friends often like the same things we do.

6

We usually know if someone is our friend. Friends make us laugh and make us feel good about ourselves. They also help us when we need it.

Our friends are special!

WHY ARE FRIENDS IMPORTANT?

Having friends is an important part of having a happy life. Friends give us **confidence**.

It's good to know that you have someone who cares about you!

Our friends are often kind and helpful. They can also play games with us and make us feel happy.

MAKING NEW FRIENDS

Everyone is different. We all look different and we all like different things. You can be friends with anyone, even if they are different from you.

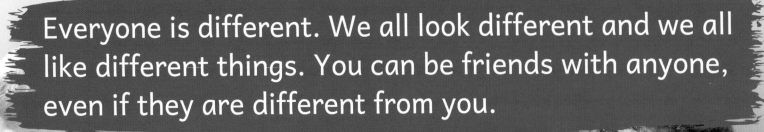

Making friends with someone can be easy. You just need to be kind and friendly.

You can learn a lot from the people you meet.

Sometimes your friends have other friends too. Your friends can help you to meet new people and make new friends.

BEING A GOOD FRIEND

Good friends respect each other. Being respectful means that we behave in a way that shows that we care about other people.

Showing people respect helps us to live and work together in a happy community. We can show respect towards other people by being polite and honest.

PEER PRESSURE

Sometimes, our friends may try to make us do something. This is called peer pressure. It can be hard to say "no" to a friend, but we always have a choice and sometimes it is important to say "no".

There may be times when you have a **disagreement** with your friends. Try to talk to them and explain how they have upset you. It is important to say sorry and make up with your friends.

LISTENING TO OTHERS

We often share our thoughts and feelings with our friends. They listen to us when we feel sad and can help to make us feel better.

Sometimes, just talking about your problems will make you feel better.

It is important that we listen to our friends. We should always show that we care about their feelings and try to help them when we can.

Top Tip: Ask a friend how they are feeling today!

MAKING FRIENDS AT SCHOOL

Going to school is a great way to meet new people and make friends. Learning and playing with others will give you the chance to get to know them.

Playing with new people at break time can be a great way to make friends.

Holly moved house and had to go to a new school. Another girl called Ashley showed Holly around and they became good friends. They love to read books, draw and sing together.

19

MAKING FRIENDS AT HOME

It is important that we are friendly towards the people that we live with at home. We can help the people that we live with by doing things around the house, such as setting the table for dinner

If you would like to help but don't know how to do something, just ask!

Tom spends time with his brother after school. They love to play football and watch their favourite television shows together.

It is important to be friendly with your **siblings**.

MAKING A DIFFERENCE

Bullying is when someone hurts another person on purpose. Bullying can make someone feel sad and scared, so it is important that you and your friends never bully anyone.

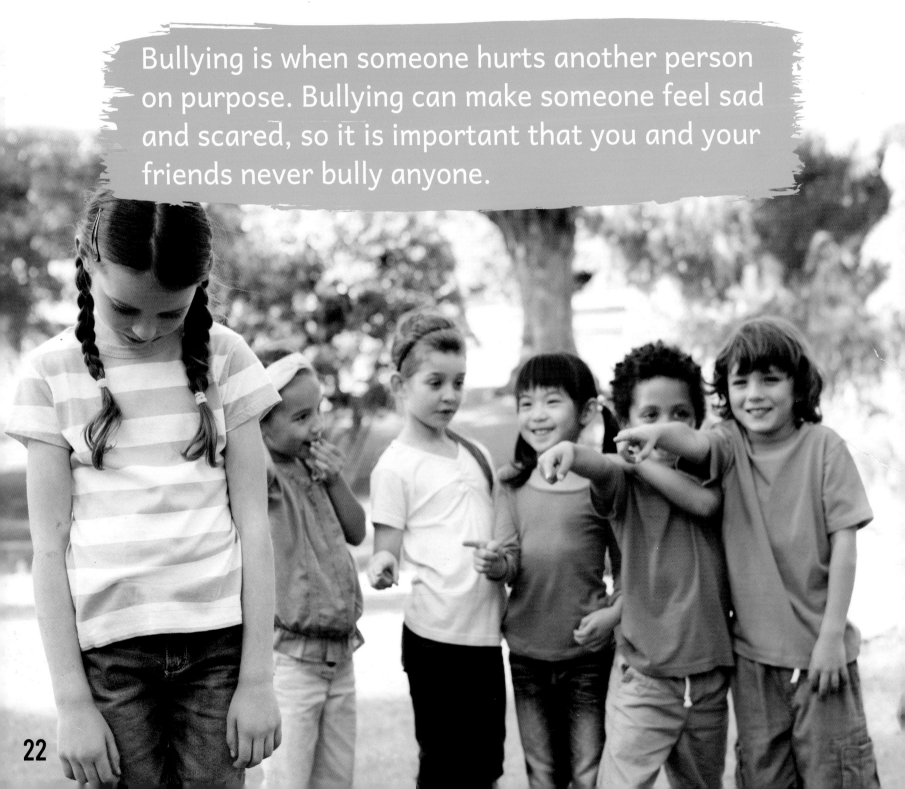

Think of all the ways that you can be a good friend and give them a go today!

Share

Be Kind

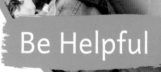

Be Helpful

Give it a go today, you could make a new friend!

Play

Be Polite

Listen

23

GLOSSARY

community	a group of people living in the same area who share similar values
confidence	a feeling that you can do something well
disagreement	an argument caused by people having different opinions
law	the rules that a community has to follow
respect	feeling that something or someone is important
responsible	to be trusted to do the right thing
siblings	brothers and sisters
trust	the belief that someone is reliable and tells the truth

INDEX

PHOTO CREDITS

Photocredits: Abbreviations: l–left, r–right, b–bottom, t–top, c–centre, m–middle.
Front Cover – gpointstudio. 2–3 – Pressmaster. 4 – Rawpixel.com. 5tl – Monkey Business Images. 5tm – Tom Wang. 5tr – Yuliya Evstratenko. 5ml – Andresr. 5mr – Romrodphoto. 5bl – Lucian Milasan. 5bm – Pressmaster. 5br – Luis Molinero. 6 – Sergey Novikov. 7 – karelnoppe. 8 – Monkey Business Images. 9 – Patrick Foto. 10 – 2xSamara.com. 11 – Pressmaster. 12 – Ilike. 13 – Phase4Studios. 14 – Dawn Shearer-Simonetti. 15 – Zurijeta. 16 – szefei. 17 – Zurijeta. 18 – Pressmaster. 19 – holbox. 20 – MJTH. 21 – racorn. 22 – wavebreakmedia. 23tl – ISchmidt. 23tm – Alinute Silzeviciute. 23tr – ISchmidt. 23bl – Syda Productions. 23bm – Pressmaster. 23br – naluwan.
Images are courtesy of Shutterstock.com. With thanks to Getty Images, Thinkstock Photo and iStockphoto.